SMALL, RECTANGULAR, REFLECTED WORLD

J.D. SCRIMGEOUR

Nixes Mate Books
Allston, Massachusetts

More Praise for *Small, Rectangular, Reflected World*

In his latest poetry collection, *Small, Rectangular, Reflected World*, J.D. Scrimgeour – Salem, MA's first poet laureate – navigates the spaces between family, memory, culture, and place. From Salem to New York to Nanjing, these poems grapple with loss, and search for meaning in a fractured world. With a plainspoken grace, he crosses the borders between grief and gratitude, drawing on such literary figures as Henry David Thoreau to Langston Hughes, and closing with a masterful meditation on 9/11. As "...every day erases the one before," Scrimgeour reminds us that even in uncertain times, there's "a sliver of joy" waiting to be found.
— **January Gill O'Neil**, author of *Glitter Road*

Before his son can speak he already knows that the ice cream Toad is rushing to give Frog will fall off the cone; a Chinese student with big dreams will squelch them, refusing to lie; and, as 9/11 proves, history doesn't repeat, it's our eternal, grim, tragic, living world. Typically, our poet here is "so full of not-knowing" [he] can hardly stand" and yet he always unflinchingly mirrors things in a way that links small stories to their vast contexts. Scrimgeour's new book is absorbing to read, and instructive to reread. Once again he shows himself to be a fresh and original writer of stalwart courage with very, very sharp eyes.
— **Alan Feldman**, author of *The Golden Coin*

Copyright © 2025 J. D. Scrimgeour

Book design by d'Entremont
Cover photograph used with permission.

All rights reserved. This book or any portion thereof may not be reproduced or used in any manner whatsoever without the express written permission of the publisher except for the use of brief quotations in a book review or scholarly journal.

ISBN 978-1-949279-60-3

Nixes Mate Books
POBox 1179
Allston, MA 02134
nixesmate.pub

For Eileen

TABLE OF

3	Savers Thrift Store, Danvers, Mass
5	Spring
7	Baseball
10	Joe & Ellen
11	Kubb
13	Graceland
15	Side Mirror
17	Roosevelt Island Tram
19	Some Questions for the Chinese Character
20	To Leave in Mandarin
22	Double Happiness
24	The Chocolate Moose
26	Pronouns

CONTENTS

Guano	29
Somewhere Outside Peking	31
The Assignment	33
Chinese Physics	34
Nanjing Subway	36
Bayonet	38
Thoreau Suite	40
Maples Seen From the Metroline	43
Notes on Revolution	44
Unsent Letter from Langston Hughes to His Father, First Semester at Columbia	46
The Never-Ending Song of the City	48
Words, Days, Flames	51

SMALL, RECTANGULAR,
REFLECTED WORLD

1 YOUR LITTLE TUSSLE

SAVERS THRIFT STORE, DANVERS, MASS

Two of the three pairs of jeans don't really fit
but I get them anyway – only five dollars,
no obvious stains, and they can go to my son,
Aidan, who is skinnier. At the checkout line
with Eileen's 62 children's books, the cashier
trusts us when we tell her the number,
and tells us we basically got the pants for free,
since we get a free book with every four,
and Eileen says the books are all going to her school,
and the cashier says great, says she bought
24 shirts herself, using her employee discount,
and brought them to the shelter. *It made my day*,
she says, and hands me our receipt...

In one of the books I bought, Gore Vidal
talks of how he became a radical:
the text of an interview from his villa in Italy
where he hosted Susan Sarandon –
her kids swam in his pool – and I wonder
if you can be a radical in a villa in Italy.
The other book I got was *Survival in Auschwitz*,
the Polish guard wiping grease from his hand
onto Primo Levi's shirt, mindlessly,
as if Levi himself was a rag.
If This is a Man was the original title.

Let's go back to children's books. How great that Eileen
got a giant Frog and Toad book for her classes,
so they will actually be able to see the pictures!
We'd read that book to Aidan before he could talk:
how Toad went to get ice cream for Frog,
but the ice cream was melting as he hurried back,
and he tripped and the cones glopped onto his head,
and no one would get to eat anything.
Aidan, hardly more than a baby, listened eagerly,
then, pages before the ice cream melted,
he'd cry and cry. We couldn't soothe him.
And slowly we came to understand
he knew how it would end,
that though he couldn't speak, he understood.

SPRING

The snow is black by now,
foot-high mountains lining the sidewalk,

and where someone failed to shovel,
I'm forced into the gravelly street.

Cars ease over the center line to avoid me,
and I feel both unsafe and powerful.

And now, again, the moment comes back:
night, and the two-lane through the center

of our small town, me in the back seat,
a car of teens. We weren't drunk,

though there were empty bottles. We knew
what we were doing when we threw them

at the hitchhikers. We gasped
at our audacity when we turned around

and drove past again, and threw more bottles,
even though one of the hitchhikers

was curled in the roadside gravel,
and the other knelt over him,

waving his arm for help. Does it matter
that I didn't throw a bottle myself,

that I asked to be taken home,
that I wept my sin to my parents,

waking them up, standing over their bed?
Thirty years ago… I slant back to the sidewalk,

my earbuds bubbling a tune,
so that the cars passing are nothing

but brushes on a snare, part
of the music, and the snow

thaws imperceptibly,
rivulets forming at the mountains' edges.

BASEBALL

Don't go to a baseball game because you want to spend time
with your aging father. You'll pay far too much for box seats,
and though David Ortiz steps from the dugout a mere ten feet away

and windmills his bats in the on-deck circle, you'll hardly notice,
wondering if you should talk more to your father,
discuss the issue of independent living. You do take a photo

of your father's face with Ortiz hulking in the background, but later,
it just reminds you how little you cared about the game,
how the photo was your attempt to make it feel special.

And don't use a baseball game as a reward, or a distraction, like years ago
when your son, in second grade, wouldn't stay in the lunch room,
having developed a phobia about the girl who would vomit after eating.

Each day he'd hide in a bathroom stall, trembling, during lunchtime.
You promised that if he stayed in the lunch room for a week straight
you'd take him to see the Sox – how he loved baseball then!

In the meantime, you'd had that run-in with the 6'5" deranged neighbor
who cast spells on your car and threw coins on your porch late at night.
You'd given him your charcoal grill as an act of friendliness, and then,

a few days later, you'd asked him to stop putting his trash out
beside yours, as if it was yours. and he erupted, stormed away
and heaved the grill over the six-foot fence into your yard.

That clang rang in your head for the next month as you wondered
what he might do next to your family. It was still ringing the night
you took your son to see the Sox lose to the Indians, 5-3.

You bought him popcorn and soda, but couldn't hold a conversation,
couldn't talk about either the game, or the lunch problem,
a light drizzle starting and stopping and starting again.

You just kept thinking how there was no solution to the neighbor,
who whittled with an ax on his front porch and glared at you,
and no solution to your son's phobia

(you'd heard he'd been sneaking back into the bathroom),
and while your son was absorbed in whether the Red Sox could rally,
you contemplated buying a gun for the first time in your life...

Now, Ortiz a colossus before you, you're still not watching the game.
Instead, you contemplate how you're situated between generations,
like a player caught on the base paths, the space between

the converging fielders rapidly shrinking until you're tagged out,
and must jog back to the shaded dugout knowing that you failed,
you fucked up, got picked off for not paying attention....

So only go to a baseball game if you intend to watch the game.
No one is playing so that your anxieties can construct absurd metaphors.
Follow the action. Note how far the runner on first takes his lead.

Does the pitcher change his motion? Think about whether to risk a steal,
down two in the seventh. Let your mind become the game's mind,
brimming with knowledge of the sport's past and present,

datum and anecdote and intuition, all this cognition in the service
of the meaningless task of winning. Watch the game.
That is what your father did. That is what your son did.

JOE & ELLEN

The winter Joe turned eighty,
they took the letters they'd written each other
when Joe was in the service,
and Ellen in nursing school in the city,
and read them to each other, sixty-year-old words
said aloud for the first time.

And when they had finished,
they shredded the letters,
and afterwards, they told their children
what they had done.

KUBB

– epithalamium

Don't mention the Kubb, Eileen said,
so the Kubb will stay out of this poem –
that game we played on the lawn in Maine
where you throw blocks at other blocks.

I won't mention that particular game
when Xanthi felt – no, was certain –
that she was right that the block
had not crossed the invisible line.

And how she shouted that she was right,
got down on her belly in the grass
to get a better angle, pointing her arm
to prove just how right she was.

I won't mention how we were all a bit surprised
at Xanthi's zeal, won't mention that Stacy
was amused at this extravagant display of passion
which is Xanthi, how she chuckled affectionately

as she slid open the screen door
to go check on the meal she and Xanthi
had planned for us. That brief,
simple chuckle reminded me

how I loved my sister, and any
irritation with how she'd brought
a moderately fun game to an abrupt,
bizarre halt dissipated into the balmy evening

and the pleasure of knowing that Stacy
knew Xanthi, too, and loved her, too.
Such generous, unflappable hosts,
these organic-beef-eating vegetarians.

Oh, the dinner was going to be delicious!
It all made me think Xanthi was probably right.

GRACELAND

Their first year in Bloomington
she and Mary were swimming to Graceland,
a game they played to make the daily laps
mean something – one or two miles a day.
How far did they get? No one remembers now.
She's raised two boys, and Mary died a decade ago.

I tried to swim, but it was even worse than running –
it was running underwater, in a narrow lane,
others bearing down on me, passing too close.
And after, my head always saturated,
nose dripping, ears useless. Ah, love.

She still swims. And, as her body
finds its way from shore to shore,
she thinks of Mary, their walk across
the twilit campus, refreshed and spent.
That time the frat boys yelled, "Get bikes,"
and Mary startled her, shouting, "Fuck you!"
Later she realized they'd said "you dykes."
We knew the world was broken then.
We just thought we could fix it.

Now, in bed on nights she's swum
I smell the pool on her – astringent, clean –
and it's as if we never left Bloomington,
the world's grime less than rumor.
She's almost an infant drifting off beside me,
and I'm almost infant, too – flesh
on flesh for comfort, for the walk into sleep.
She must have reached Memphis by now.

SIDE MIRROR

You're trying to reattach your car's side mirror,
but your ungloved fingers can't remove
the protective strip from the two-sided tape,
and the mid-morning sun angles into your eyes

as you try to align and fasten the plastic clips.
You're floundering in flashes of light and dark.
So after a few minutes you scoot inside
because January's cold, and ask your wife for help,

embarrassed you can't do even this simple task.
She peers over her glasses, studies the tape,
then returns it unstuck, separated,
and you tromp back out to the car.

Up the block you see the grown son
of the red-haired woman who, your wife heard
from the Greek grandmother across the street,
died last week. He's in a black overcoat,

standing in a crowd of cars in the driveway.
He went to school with your son.
Didn't he used to like video games?
He came into your house once or twice.

He watches you bend and futz
with a last bit of tape before you stick it
on the exterior – appearances be damned!
You wonder if grief is making this blip of image

acute for him, how years from now he might
recall that his classmate's father fixed a mirror
while he was waiting for his uncle
to come outside for the slow drive to the wake.

And you're glad that you didn't swear
too loudly about your little tussle...
She couldn't have been much older than you.
You are suddenly so full of not-knowing

you can hardly stand. In the reattached mirror
etched with silver letters, *Objects in mirror...*,
you watch him take brief, directionless steps,
in the small, rectangular, reflected world.

ROOSEVELT ISLAND TRAM

How could I not have known
about this path through the sky
for the price of a coffee?

Do I – does anyone – deserve
this calm climb, this splendid view
of the clogged bridge

and its humbled arches? Below,
the river rushes into the state,
brown as the subway.

I can't feel the wind,
and, like everywhere, people
stand around me.

A few are family.
The island I'm going to?
Just another set of city blocks.

Drawing closer, then the swift
drop, the faces looking up
at me, but not at *me*.

The glass between makes it futile
to shout my joy at what
I've seen and done. When it's over –

too soon! – I am let down,
and wander with the crowd
out the open doors and past

the field where men play soccer.
I'm back in the traffic with the pigeons.
And then I see the ferry.

SOME QUESTIONS FOR THE CHINESE CHARACTER

"The history of 也 is very complicated. It involves the confusion of three different characters." — *Reading and Writing Chinese*, William McNaughton and Li Ying

我

Is an "I" anything more
than a hand with a sword?

吗

Why do we persist in asking questions? –
horses rushing back into the burning barn.

田

Is there no path that leads
you out of your own fields?

有

What is it you want to own –
meat, or the moon?

TO LEAVE IN MANDARIN

The young Chinese women had flown through Detroit,
their luggage waylaid in Atlanta,
while they, themselves, got tested for Covid twice
in the infamous, chilly, small city of Salem.

They weren't really themselves amidst so much English,
so many why-go-wren. They'd become the why-go-wren,
eyes flickering above masks as the college van
carried them to purchase cell phones and pillows.

Did they notice the squirrels? How they were rounder,
like the Americans? Notice the gulls' careening descent
to the parking lot puddles? Did they read the mask
on the bearded man – *This is as useless as Joe Biden* –

and think about Xi Jin Ping and what would happen
if they wore a Winnie-the-Pooh mask?
Their parents, I came to learn, insist they marry.
But must they? They are always wondering.

I don't know where I am going, one ends her final essay.
I am worried, says the one who teaches me the verb to leave
and wants to become a journalist.
She has thought about her future: *I could*, she says,

as if it hurts her, *not tell all the truth, but…*
The sunny office fills with the dead air of a cell.
A parenthesis opens. Her life drifts by.
But, she says, *I will not tell a lie.*

* "why-go-wren": transliteration for the Mandarin 外国人 (foreigner)

DOUBLE HAPPINESS

for Mingyue Tao

Caught in your lashes, the sudden teardrop
Seems too heavy for your twenty years.

You're the age I was when I tutored him
in the tower of Riverside Church.
The shaky pinyin of his name spelled
his uncertainty in this new country,
all he didn't know. It must have taken
an hour to draw the handful of letters.

A card I saved. Red for luck. Double happiness.
You've told me you believe in power and money,
and you like a good romantic story,
but this old gift from my past is none of that.

I didn't even know him, you say,
and now I cry. It doesn't make sense.

女生，你不知道。
Daylight savings ushers night into afternoon
in this secluded room in the library,
where you tutor me in Mandarin.

But now we're speaking English – *It's a card*
he gave me for the Chinese New Year,
I say, *and he took me to dinner in Chinatown.*
So much food. He was as old as I am now.

A tear leaks from your eye. You brush it away,
but the one in your lash remains, quivering like mercury.

Child, you stare at that card and see the past,
the continent that man left behind, your home.
I, sons born and raised, even with my bald spot
(land-in-the-middle-of-the-sea, you taught me),
look forward. Come, speak to me – slowly! –
of your new Japanese boyfriend.
Let me try, in kindergarten Chinese,
to tell you the story I practiced:
how, years before you were born,
I fell in love in the middle of this country
that your language calls beautiful.
We can always be learning.

* 女生，你不知道。(nü sheng, ni bu zhidao):
Young woman, you do not know.

THE CHOCOLATE MOOSE

Even now, when we walk across town to get ice cream,
the steps trace backwards as well as forwards,
to the year in Bloomington when we came together
and celebrated with walks to the Chocolate Moose,
where we'd order coffee blizzards with peanut butter cups.

You reading this long after we're dead, after the U.S.
has expanded to 54 states, after the implosion,
won't likely know coffee blizzards or Bloomington.
Chocolate? Probably.

Sometimes a blizzard would be our dinner,
and we'd walk back to her room bloated,
yet still with a hunger (that happens
when you eat ice cream for dinner).
Of course, there was love, the early-days love
that made anything done together lovely:
the picnic we fended off a rabid squirrel,
the church basement production of *Hedda Gabler*,
even rushing her to the emergency room after she fainted
slicing her thumb while cutting vegetables.
When I turned and saw her slumped to the floor,
I tried to wake her, called her name, slapped her face,
saying, "This is no time to fool around."

Some days the U.S. drives us to despair,
but we shared despair then, too, holding flimsy signs
on that midwestern campus, the bank of the Jordan River,
which was really a puny creek, though
that one flash flood, it became a real river.
Two students rode inner tubes on those rapids
but lost control and – flash! – flew into the culvert,
whisked into the dark like dead leaves.

You reading this long after we're dead,
I hope you have even a sliver of the joy
we had when we heard the radio report
that the pair emerged from the darkness a mile away,
where the creek-turned-river reappeared in the world,
near the road to the softball fields, just north
of the Chocolate Moose, that mythical shack
where – even now – two lovers
lean toward the window and place their order.

PRONOUNS

I've been writing poems about things you like,
but what about the fact that you don't like poems?

Actually, you seem to like my poems in which you appear –
heroic children's librarian!

The reason you don't like poetry is why
I don't like poetry: it tries too hard:

Earnestness, pretentiousness, sledgehammer humor –
why not just hang out with a bunch of drunks?

I've got a friend who doesn't like poems that address a "you,"
The illogic of telling someone something

they already know. Even if it's something they don't know,
why share it in a poem? Why not just tell the "you"?

And if the you is dead, it's even more futile.
As Merwin's one-line poem, "Elegy," reads:

Who would I show it to?

See? My friend has a point. So...
Someone likes to garden, to swim. Someone

watches Sunday morning political shows,
even though they annoy her. Someone picks blueberries

in a state park by the ocean. And this someone
keeps me company as the world muscles in,

the sky walking by in its oblivious way,
the mayor doing her Hillary impersonation,

the streets filling with tourist gangs eager for stories
of murder and hysteria. I guess this poem didn't end up

where it intended, but when has love ever known
how to follow a map or behave?

2 NOTES ON REVOLUTION

GUANO

I wasn't planning to spend my twenties
inhaling guano dust while mining guano mountains
on a tiny island off the coast
of what will someday become Peru.

When an uncle promised work in Ningbo,
I hurried from my village, where the long hairs,
led by Jesus Christ's brother,
had ordered us not to have sex.

But in Ningbo I was put in a pen
full of shit and other young men
all talking in unknown dialects.
Then they marched us onto the clipper ship.

I saw masts clapping the air, chests
of opium balls carried down gangplanks,
and the market's fish flashing their recently living eyes,
and I realized what the ancients meant by beauty.

But then we went into the hold, where the fuckers
– barbarians? white men?– peed on us though the hatches
because some of us bitched about the state of things,
and, when we didn't stop, poured boiling water on us.

We lit fires – why not? – and, well, that didn't help things.
I was lying, diseased, surrounded by dead men.
Footsteps. Different barbarians came, and put
those still alive on another white man's boat,

and brought us here. Have I mentioned they had guns?
And now have these Africans
driving us with whips, making sure
we cart our quota of birdshit.

Occasionally, in those moments when I'm pushing
the unloaded cart back to the mountain,
and the lesser weight gives me a chance to reflect,
I imagine someone a few centuries from now

telling my story at a coffeehouse in Cambridge
to, oh, seventeen people. Wouldn't that be interesting?

SOMEWHERE OUTSIDE PEKING

I was in bad shape. I could hardly cry.
I was probably a girl. I was probably
missing a limb, or a lung. To be honest,

lying in that alley, I was fine calling it quits.
But the missionaries, who kept track
of village pregnancies, found me.

They brought me to the monastery
and rushed through my baptism
before my final breath.

The water was a new sensation.
It made me want to live.
But then I died. I was dead.

And buried in the small Christian graveyard.
You know when you think a story's over,
and though it wasn't good, at least it's over?

When the villagers dug me up, and beat
two of the priests to death,
I wasn't grateful for their companionship.

They just buried me again in their graveyard.
Their silence, as they flung dirt on me,
felt like it meant something.

The priests had nothing to say to me,
even though we had death in common,
and though I hadn't been around long,

I could see things were just going to get uglier.
I would have been happy with two arms
and a heart that worked. A chance at life.

Despite it all, though, there was this:
When the church windows' colored light
touched my eyes before I succumbed,

it wasn't like a god exactly, but it gave me
a moment of wonder, which I guess
could be called happiness.

THE ASSIGNMENT

for Nien Cheng

Write your autobiography,
they said, everyone in the country
has done it, and they handed me
a roll of paper
and returned me to my cell,

where I watched the spider stumble
across the floor and crawl
under the cement toilet.
The weather had turned cold.

I'd spent months watching it
diligently loop its web –
perfectly symmetrical –
across the corner of the room.

Now, it seemed too feeble
to climb the wall. Above me,
the detached web waved its strands.
I began to write
as little as possible.

CHINESE PHYSICS

There is No 'Chinese Physics'
– Fang Lizhi

I helped build an A-bomb calculating on an abacus,
then they ordered me to live in a village and dig wells.

The peasants taught me: I took a shot of grain alcohol,
stripped in frozen January, and was lowered 30 feet,
where, using only my arms, I filled buckets with wet sand
that was hauled up and emptied. Some sloshed out
and rained on me – fat, grainy, icy teardrops.

Before I could return to being a professor,
they sent me to the coal mine in Bagong Mountain.
I would crawl, searching for a vein.
It was so hot and so black, I thought of Dante.
Again I was naked, this time to lessen the heat
that came from the ancient depths of the earth.

There is a logic clear as the night sky
that explains how my life brought me to astrophysics,
and how I find myself hidden away
after Tiananmen, windows locked and covered.
For thirteen months, we have not seen the sky.

Who is we, you ask? Li Shuxian
is with me in this shuttered house – two physicists
who long ago, when the party expelled her,
agreed to "freeze" our love. I cannot explain,
even today, what precisely that meant,
but our love, to exist, had to exist those years
outside of space and time.

In the mines of Bagong, the shovels clanked
against coal, the conveyor belt churned.
You dug from one blackness to the next,
naked bodies in front of you wriggling forward
toward somewhere deeper, somewhere even blacker.

Back when I was lifted, shivering, from the well,
I only hoped I had not stayed down too long,
that my legs would not be forever cold and numb.
I clothed myself, took another shot of grain alcohol.

As a villager who had made the descent,
I had the honor of eating white-flour pancakes.

NANJING SUBWAY

The sugary edible paper
around the glazed strawberries
in the Fuzimiao district,
next to the boat tours,
and across from the Confucian temple,
was not eaten by the students
who took us for Peking Duck,
where a table whirled dishes,
and Chinese opera fluttered
from the room's center.

There probably is no crime
that has not been committed
in this city today,
Minnie Vautrin wrote
as she shielded civilians
on Ginling's campus. Today,
cats lean as facts stalk
leafy walkways, nibble
piles of rice left
on a low wall by
an unseen hand. They carry
their bundle of bone and fur,
unafraid of the human animal.

Their thin frames hold
more history than the state-
sponsored memorial
that dominates blocks
of the city: with its giant
sculpture of a severed head,
and everywhere, 300,000,
a number the government feels
it must establish, rendered
in English, Mandarin, German...
Vautrin, back in Indiana
in '41, ran her gas stove
until she stopped seeing.

The new subway system
is cleaner and faster than any
in America.
The park under the bridge
famous today for its suicides,
where the Yangtze pushes through
like people on a forced march,
has been closed for a year.
We were only there a month.
We never saw the river.

BAYONET

"Once my mother said, 'It's an ancient place, it's not really around anymore.'
Where had it gone?" — from Peter Balakian's *Black Dog of Fate*

How present they are. A handful of coins
the Armenian girl hid in her "secret place"
during the death march
                              glint underneath
today's foggy rain, the lamb stew
and ranking proposals for a poetry festival
and the winter trees like a lost army
in the thick mist.

She hid them before her mother,
too weak to move, lay on the dry plateau
and told her children to go on:
"I have lived my life," she said,

before her brother died in the cave
where the gendarmes set people aflame,

before a gendarme woke her and pissed
on her face, before the night she was raped,
before she was "rescued" by the Kurdish nomad

while she slept –
                        she awoke and lived with him
five years, bore two children, then escaped.

No one waits for us as we leave the country house,
our stew-stained bowls left in the sink,
and walk through the mist across the gravel
to our beat-up poet cars...
                                the woods drip around us
dark grey bars against the day's grey.
I can't see twenty yards away.

Is this history? The way the dogs, frisky,
moved around us so rapidly
we accidentally stepped on them?
How they didn't seem to mind?

The gendarmes would point a gun
and order an Armenian to shit, then
poke the steaming feces with their bayonets,
or even, sometimes, use their hands,
                                  searching for coins.

THOREAU SUITE

Before it was the Concord, it was the Musketaquid,
or Grass-Ground river, and after it is the Concord
it will be a grass-ground river, and after that
it will be river, and the trees will angle
toward some patch of sun, their trunks
sunk in a current that's so slow it's like time,
so slow that when snow lands on it
it simply stops a moment, thinking, before it chooses
to melt, and before all that, it was a river,
and before that it was water and before that
there were no words and before that

*

Every day the trees write on the sky,
the dead bracken writes on the snow,
the egret sculpts the mist,
the chipmunk carves the pine needles,
and the milk snake sketches on the sleepy stream.

These are poems, these scratches
and explorations, these leavings

and shadows.

*

If the hand moves gently,
the bream, guarding its spawn,
may be petted – it will nibble
at fingers – and may even be
lifted out of the water,
if the hand moves gently
underneath and closes the fingers
gradually, moving
as slowly as the current,

the bream, guarding its spawn,
may be lifted to the surface

and then, out
of the water.

Henry did this.

*

After the skitter and the shuffle,
as the darkness again settles,
the silence is not the same silence,
but stiller, and more alert,

and the darkness is not
the same darkness, something
has moved in it. Reach your hand
out until you can't see it,

can't know what it is you'll touch.
You can only know a muskrat
has been in your potatoes,
or was that a fox, its shock

of red buried in the night,
or was it a black bear,
and where is your gun,
and why?

MAPLES SEEN FROM THE METROLINE

They cower in the wind of the silver train,
then right themselves, the terror
lingering in their sudden lightness
from the starlings' startled departures.

A backhoe's diseased yellow widens
the gully to lay more tracks,
gouging roots, lifting rocks,
setting all in the dump truck's pit.

When you are bound to the ground,
there's no self-determination,
except maybe in the seeds' leap
into the unsettled air, their hunt for earth

amid islands of plastic and cement.
Why should they trust, when even as a boy
I peeled bark from the sycamore
that signaled I was nearly home?

NOTES ON REVOLUTION

I asked if he'd rather blow up institutions
or build them. He said:
I'd rather work inside institutions
to make them crumble.

*

Stay in your lane, they say.
But what if I'm on foot –
what if I just want to get across
the goddamned street?

*

I don't know if God loves me,
but Whitman does.

*

Sometimes I worry that
the self isn't that important,
and that doubt, self-questioning,
is all solipsistic,
and there are some injustices
I could help right...

then I wake in the morning
and pick up the sprung mousetrap
in the corner of the kitchen,
the small dead creature
with its neck snapped,
its black eye swollen to bursting,
the chip of peanut it never tasted...
and I get a plastic bag –
something I should be recycling –
drop the corpse inside, trap, peanut and all,
and toss it in the garbage.

*

Explain this: most people I agree with
about politics annoy me.

*

Richard Wright believed
the Communist Revolution was inevitable
and good, glorious even,
and he saw no place for his doubting self
in that world to come.

UNSENT LETTER FROM LANGSTON HUGHES TO HIS FATHER, FIRST SEMESTER AT COLUMBIA

Father,
There is no place like New York.
So many cultures, the Italians, the Negroes, the Jews.
I know you want me to study, but the shows
are better than any lecture.
And have you heard jazz? The shining
rivers of the soul! Still, there's the moment
when I get directed to the peanut gallery
that I recall your wish I go to college in Munich.
You asked me why live like a black man
when I don't have to.

New York's expensive.
The food they serve in the cafeteria
has no taste, and the university
makes me eat in my room.
They weren't even going to give me a room
when they discovered that I was "colored,"
so school is not without its inconveniences.
But I'm passing all my subjects.

I'm grateful for your support, and if you could see a way
to send fifty dollars, it would get me through the semester,
and let me buy a ticket to Mexico City.
I would start working right away.
I know you hate idleness.
I'd earn my ticket back
and some pocket money for the spring.

Today on the subway, the car filled with white men
heading downtown to where the money is,
and though the car was crowded,
none dared take the seat beside me.
So you see, father, why I like this city:
a negro can live like a king.

THE NEVER-ENDING SONG OF THE CITY

for Alicia

You leave the train with such joy
that your dress smiles with flowers,
and Wen, the boy from China
who works sixty hours a week
in the mall's food court,
holds your hand. Was it the day
you began to learn his language,
how to write the ideograph
for friend, that those years
began to slough away? – hunched
in school hallways, K-pop
popping through earbuds,
your Puerto Rican mother's
admonitions – *it's not your culture* –
haunting you just as school
haunted you. Class after class
you wouldn't, couldn't speak,
head tucked into your chest.
They said you needed to do this
to become a success.

That's all at your back now,
a train stop in the past,
and as you nearly skip
past the conductor, you notice
the newly planted blueberry bush
between the platform and canal.
The chemicals poured in the river
before your ancestors came
can't ruin these blueberries,
but you'll have to share them
with the starlings (another immigrant).
Wen is so tall! His head almost as high
as the grand heads of the Chinese Zodiac
on the Rose Kennedy Greenway.
The dragon and snake extend
their tongues to taste the market's
waft of ripe fruit. As you take
the long route through the park to Chinatown,
still holding hands, the foxglove,
roses and poppies raise their fists.

3 WORDS, DAYS, FLAMES

WORDS, DAYS, FLAMES

At the National September 11 Memorial Museum, a stark wall separates visitors from a repository containing about 8,000 unidentified human remains.

On the wall, commemorating those who died in the attack, is a 60-foot-long inscription in 15-inch letters made from the steel of the twin towers: "No day shall erase you from the memory of time. Virgil."

It sounds fitting – except in the context of Book Nine of the *Aeneid*, from which it is translated. There, a reader learns who Virgil is commemorating, who his "you" are.

"You" are not nameless. You are Nisus and Euryalus.

"You" do not number in the thousands. You are two.

"You" are not civilians. You are Trojan soldiers.

"You" have not been thrown together by cruel chance. You are a loving pair.

Your deaths are not unprovoked. You have just slaughtered the enemy in an orgy of violence, skewering soldiers whom you ambushed in their sleep. For this, the enemy has killed you and impaled your heads on spears.

— Adapted from "A Memorial Inscription's Grim Origins," David W. Dunlop, *New York Times*, April 2, 2014

*

Some days the sky's so deep and unfathomably blue
it seems to contain all the world's memories
and all its dreams.
                    September 11th.
Not the towers melting, not the panic,
the pink mist in the streets, but the waking,
and driving our children to school,
returning home to make love.
The morning air with its nip of autumn,
that soul-stinging blue sky, almost
too rich to be in the bedroom, though
the windows were open, the music
of the morning melding with our music.

*

                                  My friends were gone.
      Some spent with toil, some with despair oppressed
      Leap'd headlong from the heights, the flames consumed the rest.
              — Bk. 2, *The Aeneid,* (trans. Dryden)

It must be true, yes? There were witnesses.
Two people – who they were, no one knows –
held hands before they leapt from the tower
and the flames that had chased them to the edge…
The first time I held hands with a girl

I was twelve, walking a middle school hallway
How long since that touch and this one –
my pen scrolling across the page
in a Lynn, Massachusetts deli
scrawling and crossing out words
while the customers and proprietor
speak Spanish and a heavy metal band
in the basement apartment shakes the floorboards –

How long after Dido's pyre until Virgil
picked up his pen and scrawled
No day shall erase you from the memory of time ?
How long after she stepped up and up,
climbing the fine gifts she had given him
bare feet sinking into the rich clothing,
bruising on the hard treasures:
goblets, plates, all that would soon be blackened,
all that would soon be smoke, flakes of grey ash.

The pyre built with all she had given him,
every vestment, every treasure,
the jeweled sword she drove into her chest.

    And Virgil, at his court appointed desk,
conjuring the flame and the tears, the ships
easing into the horizon, Aeneas's grimace.

In that span between deed and word, the births
and funerals, the legions of warriors, the lives
of citizens, slaves, courtesans, artisans,
between the ship's last look backward
at the fire, and Virgil's look at the fire.

*

> The quote speaks to the indelibility of our memories. In selecting this quote, our focus was not on the specific narrative of the classic story nor its characters.
> – Alice M. Greenwald, Museum Director

Remember me, remember me.
Forget my fate, but ah! Remember me.
— "Dido's Lament" in Henry Purcell's opera,
Dido and Aeneas, librettist Nahum Tate

No day shall erase you from the memory of time?
No day shall save you from the anonymity of time.

*

What fun to live in an Empire.
You feel superior, you can afford guilt.
You look at places with no clean water,
at places where food is scarce,
and you say, "There but for the grace..."
and then you run your road race
or text your friend about her date.

You buy organic food, or Burger King.
You write an angry poem or two.
We all desire to live in an Empire.
So much is done for you!

*

So, let's sneak over
cut the watchman's throat
then kill as many as we can
while they're sleeping,
and by the way, you know
I love you.

After they had snuck into the enemy camp,
and slaughtered several in their sleep,
drawing blood from body parts I'd never known –
a weazon? a brainpan? –

they hurried back, but the glint
of a stolen helmet gave them away.
More death. That's the story here.
And Virgil with his promise to commemorate.

D'ya ever wonder
if, long after we're dead,
they'll think we all believed
that shit about gods,
the underworld, the lies

we're born into? Those
poor superior saps —
I wonder if they'll evolve
so they don't regret killing.

*

> Erect a lofty pile, expos'd in air.
>   — *The Aeneid,* Dido's directions

As my father taught me, I built a cone of twigs,
with larger thicker branches crossing above,
then crumpled yesterday's newspaper, eased it
underneath, struck a match, and watched
the flame flare high and orange,
watched the twigs catch and twist in the heat,
drop, black, to the ground, the branches
not catching, the fire fading to flicker, to spark,
then out. I can never keep it lit.

*

> When a match is struck, the friction caused by the glass powder rubbing together produces enough heat to turn the red phosphorus into white phosphorus, which catches fire in air. This small amount of heat starts a chemical reaction that uses the oxidizing agent to produce oxygen gas. The heat and oxygen gas then cause the sulfur to burst into flame.

> A "strike anywhere" match works similarly, but instead of phosphorus being on a striking surface, it is added to the head of the match. You can tell the difference between the two types of matches by looking at the colors of the match heads.
> — Adapted from Michigan State University's
> *Ask Science Theatre*

The plane, the match; the building, the strip.
No, the building the match; the sky the strip.
No, the words, the match; the mind, the strip.
What is it, to be inside a matchhead?
(What was it, to be inside those planes?)
What is inside your head?

Do you remember Virgil?
Do you remember Aeneas?
Do you, for as long as you live,
say the names of those who died in the towers?
Do you recall Nisus and Euryalus?
Do you know what they did?

We lie.

*

> Today, like every other day, we wake up empty
> and frightened. — Rumi

That September my sons and I
spent hours in our small backyard.

I flipped balls into the sky,
and they ran, they leapt, they dove.
A quiet sky – the bobbing branches,
a corner of the neighbor's house,
some clouds, sparrows and grackles.
The empty sky felt too blue,
no streaming contrails, and the world
seemed less connected, the people
in New York, DC, the people
in Afghanistan were almost imaginary,
people in a dream who
I could not quite envision.
What was here was what we had:
a tennis ball, a dirt backyard,
two boys in dusty shorts; their reedy voices
tinged the afternoon with – yes – joy.

*

> The best advice is what any old con will tell you:
> walk slow, drink a lot of water.
> — William Wantling

And so, those weeks after, I walked slow
and stayed hydrated. Each morning
with my bowl of raisin bran,
I poured myself a glass of water.
And each morning, my stomach would resist.

I'd eat a few bites then sigh.
For over a month: a few spoonfuls
of cereal every morning, then I'd stop,
appetite gone. News of anthrax
and Afghanistan bubbled from the radio.
And then one day – did some god intervene? –
it struck me: water with cereal tastes awful.

*

My Uncle worked in Veteran's Affairs,
a building down the street from the towers.
What he saw out his window I've never asked.
Weeks after, he could hardly leave his room,
and then one day he and a friend –
a Muslim friend – volunteered together,
passing out sandwiches to the laborers
down near the wreckage, breathing in
contaminated air. Simple, mindless work,
plain conversation, until the day became
any busy day in the city, and he felt better.

*

No day shall erase you… What's a day?
A revolution, turning toward, then away.
And every day erases the one before.
Every second one more step away
from the act, one more chance to revise.

Virgil, nobody cares about you.
Let's just erase your name, let the words stand alone,
metal letters fastened to the stone.
No day shall erase you from the memory of time
They're not your words anyway, but the translator's,
And in Dryden's version it's about fame, not forgetting:
"Your fame shall ever live," he – Virgil? Dryden? – promises.

They'll take your words to do their work.
The dead, who just were going about their day,
turned to heroes, warriors, the famed,
and used to spur the country to war
against – who? It really didn't matter.

ACKNOWLEDGEMENTS

The Assignment: *Solstice*
Baseball: *Sport Literate*
Bayonet: *Tar River Poetry*
Joe & Ellen: *Stockmal Memorial Reading Broadside, 2023*
The Never-Ending Song of the City: *Lily Poetry Review*
Savers Thrift Store, Danvers, Mass: *Lily Poetry Review*
Side Mirror: *The Common*
Some Questions for the Chinese Character: *Artsfuse*
Spring: *Nixes Mate Review*

Thanks to Alan Feldman and Richard Hoffman for their help with these poems.

This book couldn't have been written without the support of the Salem Writers Group and the Thursday Poets, as well as the Salem Athenaeum, Salem State University, and the city of Salem.

Thanks, also to January Gill O'Neil and Heather Treseler for their endorsements.

Much love and gratitude to my parents, James and Christine Scrimgeour, and to Eileen, Aidan, and Guthrie.

And finally, thanks to Michael McInnis and Annie Pluto at Nixes Mate for believing in this book and finding the perfect look for it.

ABOUT THE AUTHOR

J.D. Scrimgeour is the author of five poetry collections, including the bilingual 香蕉面包 *Banana Bread*, *Lifting the Turtle* and *The Last Miles*. He won the Association of Writers and Writing Program's (AWP) Award for Nonfiction for his second book of nonfiction, *Themes for English B: A Professor's Education In & Out of Class*. With musician Philip Swanson he released *Ogunquit & Other Works*, a CD blending music and poetry. In 2025, he began his term as the inaugural Poet Laureate of Salem, Massachusetts.

42° 19' 47.9" N 70° 56' 43.9" W

Nixes Mate is a navigational hazard in Boston Harbor used during the colonial period to gibbet and hang pirates and mutineers.

Nixes Mate Books features small-batch artisanal literature, created by writers who use all 26 letters of the alphabet and then some, honing their craft the time-honored way: one line at a time.

nixesmate.pub

www.ingramcontent.com/pod-product-compliance
Lightning Source LLC
Chambersburg PA
CBHW060540080526
44586CB00012B/806